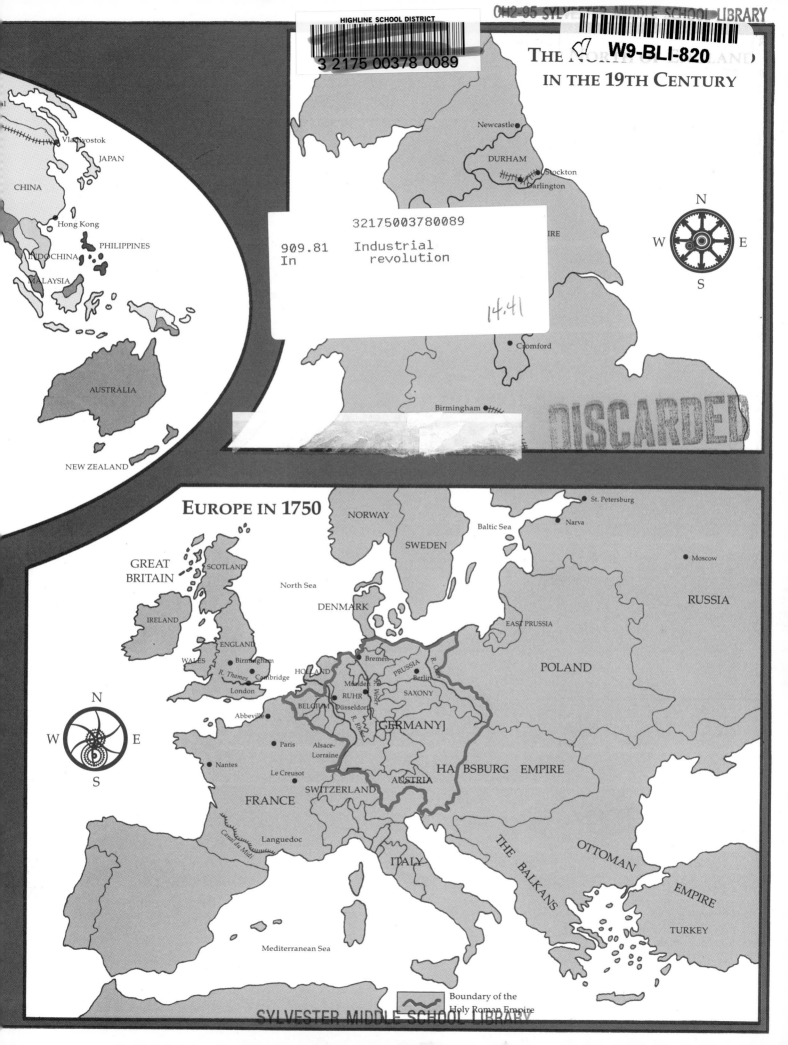

THE NORTH OF ENGLAND IN THE 19TH CENTURY

Newcastle

DURHAM

Stockton
Darlington

IRE

Cromford

Birmingham

N
W   E
S

Vladivostok

JAPAN

CHINA

Hong Kong

PHILIPPINES

INDOCHINA

MALAYSIA

AUSTRALIA

NEW ZEALAND

EUROPE IN 1750

NORWAY

St. Petersburg

Baltic Sea

Narva

SWEDEN

Moscow

GREAT
BRITAIN

SCOTLAND

North Sea

DENMARK

EAST PRUSSIA

RUSSIA

IRELAND

ENGLAND

POLAND

WALES

Birmingham

Bremen

PRUSSIA

R.

R. Thames   Cambridge

HOLLAND

Berlin

London

Munden

SAXONY

BELGIUM

Düsseldorf

RUHR

R. Rhine

Abbeville

[GERMANY]

N
W   E
S

Paris

Alsace-
Lorraine

HABSBURG   EMPIRE

Nantes

Le Creusot

AUSTRIA

SWITZERLAND

FRANCE

Canal du Midi

Languedoc

ITALY

THE BALKANS

OTTOMAN

EMPIRE

TURKEY

Mediterranean Sea

Boundary of the
Holy Roman Empire

INDUSTRIAL
REVOLUTION

LIVING HISTORY

INDUSTRIAL
REVOLUTION

JOHN D. CLARE, Editor

GULLIVER BOOKS
HARCOURT BRACE & COMPANY
SAN DIEGO   NEW YORK   LONDON

HARCOURT BRACE

First published in Great Britain in 1993 by The Bodley Head
Children's Books

First U.S. edition 1994

Library of Congress Cataloging-in-Publication Data
Industrial revolution/John D. Clare, editor. — 1st U.S. ed.
p.   cm. — (Living history)
"Gulliver books."
Summary: Describes the dramatic technological, industrial, and so-
cial changes brought about by the Industrial Revolution in America
and Europe.
ISBN 0-15-200514-5
1. Industry — History — Juvenile literature. [1. Industry — History.
2. United States — Industries — History. 3. Europe — Industries —
History.] I. Clare, John D., 1952–   . II. Series: Living history (San
Diego, Calif.)
HD2321.I53   1994
909.81 — dc20   93-2554

Printed and bound in China

A B C D E

Director of Photography Tymn Lintell
Photography Charles Best
Production Manager, Photography Fiona Nicholson
Designer Dalia Hartman
Visualizer Anthony Parks
Typesetting Thompson Type, San Diego, California
Reproduction Scantrans, Singapore

ACKNOWLEDGMENTS

Historical Advisor: Derek McKay, London School of Economics. **Cast-
ing**: Baba's Crew. **Costumes**: Val Metheringham. **Makeup**: Emma Scott,
Jane Jamieson. **Picture Research**: Lesley Coleman. **Props**: Cluny South.
Transport: Peter Knight, Road Runner Film Services. **Maps and Time-
line**: John Laing. **Map Illustrations**: David Wire.

Additional Photographs: Archiv für Kunst und Geschichte, Berlin, p. 37
(left). Association of American Railways, Washington, D.C., pp. 28–29.
Beamish, p. 19. Susan Benn, pp. 38–39. Bridgeman Art Library, p. 18 (top,
National Railway Museum, York). The British Library, p. 63 (bottom).
Deutsche Fotothek, Dresden, p. 47. E. T. Archive, p. 40 (bottom). Mary
Evans Picture Library, p. 17 (top), p. 23, p. 26 (top), p. 40 (top). GEC-
Marconi, p. 37 (right). Hanwell Community Center, pp. 46–47. Histo-
rische Archiv der Fried, Krupp AG, Essen, p. 7 (right). The Hulton
Deutsch Collection, p. 26 (bottom). The Illustrated London News Picture
Library, p. 53. Manchester Public Libraries, p. 63 (top). The Mansell Col-
lection, p. 63 (middle). Masson Mills, Derbyshire, front cover (back-
ground). Museum of the City of New York, The Byron Collection, p. 43.
National Archives, Still Picture Branch, Washington, D.C., pp. 58–59.
National Museum of Wales, p. 30 (bottom). By permission of the Keeper
of the National Railway Museum, York, p. 57 (top). Rensselaer Polytech-
nic Institute, Archives, Folsom Library, N.Y., p. 33 (exterior detail, photograph by Irving Underhill). Royal Geographical Society, pp. 40–41.
Trustees of the Science Museum, p. 22, p. 54 (middle l. to r. 2, 3, 4;
bottom l. to r. 1, 3). Scientific American, Oct. 15, 1853, plan by James
Swett, p. 29 (top). T. H. Shepherd, p. 7 (left). Trades Union Congress
Library, p. 48. Courtesy of the Board of Trustees of the V&A, painting by
Samuel Scott, p. 10.

Contents

The Old Order

On August 17, 1896, Bridget Driscoll became the first person to be killed by a motorcar in London. The vehicle was traveling at 4 miles (6 kilometers) per hour. It so amazed and terrified the 44-year-old woman that she stood transfixed in its path until it knocked her down.

Today the world has changed. Accidents still happen, but cars are commonplace, mass-produced by robots. Food comes from all over the world to your local supermarket; in many places you can pay by presenting a piece of plastic at the checkout counter. On television you can watch events as they happen at any time of day or night.

The most amazing change of all has been in the rate of change itself. The astounding sequence of events that shaped the modern industrial world began only 200 years ago and covers only 1/2,000th of the history of the human race. Today we expect continuous improvement in technology and wealth; inventions and innovations come faster and faster, and we can barely keep up.

AMERICA IN THE 18TH CENTURY

The first official United States census, taken in 1790, showed that more than 3.9 million people lived in the new nation. Of those people, more than 80 percent worked on or owned farms. Most farming families lived at subsistence level — producing just enough to feed themselves — although some large plantations in the South employed and fed many people.

For many Americans the turn of the century was a time of great opportunity. When America, long a colony under British rule, won the Revolutionary War (1775–1783), all male property owners were given the right to vote. Eventually property requirements were eliminated, so even poor men could have a say in their country's government (women, though, still had to wait for that right).

The revolution also gave common people the chance to buy land confiscated from pro-British families or to farm a homestead on land newly released by the peace treaty. Immigrants, attracted by the availability of land and the need for labor, flocked from Europe to America. Some came as indentured servants, tied to a master for whom they would work for several years in order to pay back their travel costs and other debts.

Times were not so bright for the African American slaves who made up 18 percent of the population, however. Despite much debate among politicians, the American Revolution did not free them, and they remained tied to their white owners.

EUROPE IN THE 18TH CENTURY

In Europe in 1790, little seemed to have changed since the Middle Ages. The population was perhaps 145 million. Here, too, the majority of people lived at subsistence level, on farms in rural areas. During times of plenty, the population might grow, but eventually war, famine, or disease would force the numbers back down.

Most of the states of Europe were the private inheritances of individual ruling families. Germany, under the weakening Holy Roman Empire, was divided into some 350 principalities, duchies, counties, and bishoprics. To the east, the Ottoman and Habsburg emperors controlled huge empires and believed that they had a "divine right" to rule their countries however they wished. Ordinary people had little or no say in government.

In most countries, wealth and power were concentrated in the hands of the nobility — at most, perhaps 2 percent of the population. In Hungary the Estherhazy family owned 13,500 square miles (35,000 square kilometers) of land, an area the size of present-day Holland. In contrast, millions of ordinary people were serfs; they were forced to live on their lord's estate and were reckoned as part of its equipment. Serfdom was common in Russia, Germany, and the Habsburg Empire. Serfs could not marry or leave the village without permission, and they had to work, unpaid, for a number of days each week on their lord's estate.

INDUSTRIAL CHANGE

Most industry in Europe and America was on a small scale in 1790, since most people worked at home. The biggest glassworks in the Habsburg Empire employed only 40 workers. Large factories — such as the Van Robais textile mill at Abbeville in France, which had 3,000 employees — were rare.

Customs barriers and poor conditions hindered trade. On the River Weser in Germany, there were 22 separate tolls between Münden and Bremen. As each stop took at least an hour while the barge's entire cargo was inspected, a boat captain would waste a whole day simply paying tolls. Although some European roads were improved and some canals were built during the 18th century, traffic still moved at the speed of the horse. In America years of warfare had left roads in poor condition due to neglect. In 1790 it took a stagecoach three days to travel the 250 miles (400 kilometers) from New York City to Boston, Massachusetts.

But sometime late in the 18th century the changes that would bring the Industrial Revolution began. Britain experienced a "takeoff" into economic growth. During the following century, industrialization

spread and similar "takeoffs" occurred in the United States, Belgium, France, and Germany. Industry replaced agriculture as the main economic activity in these countries. Machines began to replace human skill and power, iron took over wood's role as the most important building material, and coal replaced wood as the most important fuel. Trade increased, and transport and communication developed. The capital stock (machines and buildings) grew, and institutions developed to finance the new enterprises. Living and working conditions changed rapidly — sometimes for the better, sometimes for the worse — and people's responses to them in turn changed governments and entire societies.

Above left: Barges pass through the Regent's Canal in London in the 19th century. The locks can be sealed at either end by miter gates. Water is then allowed to flow in or out so that the barges can go up or down hills. Above: "Fritz," the huge steam-hammer installed at the Krupp steelworks in Germany in 1861.

The Domestic System

In the 18th century, most manufactured goods were produced by hand, in people's homes. In some areas, such as the West Riding of Yorkshire in the north of England, clothiers made their pieces of cloth during the week and sold them on Saturdays at a local market known as Piece Hall. In other areas, including much of America, families that could not afford the raw materials got them from a businessman called a "putter-out," who then collected the finished product and paid for their labor at the end of the week. In Languedoc in the south of France, a putter-out called Goudard employed 6,000 spinners and weavers. The domestic system suited the employer, who did not have to lay out money to build a factory.

Beyond France and Britain, European industry struggled or failed altogether. In Germany it was restricted by powerful guilds, as it had been since the Middle

Ages. In countries farther east there was almost no industry at all. Some unscientific observers blamed the local people. Polish industry was insignificant, claimed the German traveler vom Stein in 1781, "because the ordinary Pole is a careless being who lives miserably and who knows no joy but wild living and drunkenness."

The whole family takes part in cloth making. One daughter (center) brushes the cotton between two carding brushes, to straighten the fibers into roving (thick bands of unspun fibers). The mother and an elder daughter (right) do the spinning. While the grandmother (left) winds thread, the father weaves cloth on a hand loom, and the son tends the fire and watches a baby in a cradle.

Although it is hard work — even the children often put in long hours — family members can start and stop working when they wish.

When industry is thriving, the family spends a lot of time making cloth; when times are hard, they pay more attention to farming their small plot of land, if they have one. During bad economic times, children might also work as servants in wealthier homes.

A tub in the corner is used to collect the family's urine, which they sell (at a penny a tub) to the local cloth mill, where it is used as a bleach.

Trade and Growth

In the second half of the 18th century, manufacturing in Britain began to change. Machine power began to replace human muscle, and work moved out of the home and into the factory.

As businessmen invested their money in the new machines and factories, they employed more workers. When workers spent their wages on manufactured goods, businessmen made a profit. They in turn invested these profits in their business, paying wages to more workers — who then bought goods, and so on. In this way businessmen and workers together created a cycle of economic growth that eventually became self-sustaining.

What caused this takeoff? Looking for an answer, scholars have suggested many causes. Perhaps improvements in agriculture in the 18th century reduced the cost of food, so people had money left over to buy manufactured goods. Perhaps the period of the British Civil War (1642–1660) broke down class barriers, so that aristocrats were not ashamed to invest in industry (which they considered less "noble" than owning land). Did the religious reformation of the 16th century create a "business ethic"? Some historians have traced the Industrial Revolution's origins back to a burst of new ideas in the 13th century! Others suggest that the takeoff was caused by a freak combination of all these factors.

Workers at a London warehouse unload chests of tea and bales of cotton, weighing the goods and recording their arrival. In the mid-18th century Britain's empire includes large areas of America and India. The Navigation Laws of 1651 and 1660 forbid the colonies to manufacture finished goods, and they have to buy their machinery, cloth, and luxuries from Britain. The colonies must send their produce — raw materials such as sugar, tobacco, coffee, cotton, and flax — to Britain. Tobacco, for example, can be legally shipped only to England, where officials tax it and then reexport up to seven-eighths of a shipment to other countries, earning a higher profit for Britain.

Between 1700 and 1772 the value of trade between Britain and her colonies quadruples to nearly £14 million ($56 million) a year. This trade stimulates the British economy and creates a wealthy merchant class there with money to invest, while Americans increasingly resent British control. In 1774 angry Americans will organize a boycott of British goods.

Above: *The busy East India Wharf in London.*

Inventions and Innovation

The first industry to mechanize in Britain was the cotton industry. The breakthrough was the innovation (first use) of the flying shuttle, soon after its invention in 1733; this type of shuttle let weavers pass horizontal threads quickly through the vertical threads on the loom.

Using the flying shuttle, weavers could work much faster than before, so they needed more spun thread; it now took eight spinners to supply one weaver. A number of attempts were made, therefore, to invent a better spinning machine and thus increase the amount of thread each spinner made available. Between 1764 and 1767 James Hargreaves developed the spinning jenny, a machine with many spindles instead of just one. In 1769 Richard Arkwright, a wigmaker, patented the spinning frame, which produced thread by using rollers turning at different speeds. In 1779 Samuel Crompton patented the spinning mule, which combined the moving carriage of Hargreaves's jenny with the rollers of Arkwright's frame. By 1812 there were thousands of mule machines, powering 5 million spindles. The new spinning machines were powered by water wheels and, in an increasing number of cases, steam engines.

For a while, there was a glut of thread. In 1820 there were a quarter of a million weaving looms in use, but even with their flying shuttles they were not sufficient to deal with the vast amounts of machine-spun thread. Hand-loom weavers prospered. They were sure that their job could not be mechanized. But Edmund Cartwright had already invented a primitive power loom, which was innovated in the 1830s.

Domestic workers hated and dreaded the new machines. The hand-loom weavers found themselves "clothed in rags . . . sleeping on straw . . . working 16 hours a day," as they tried to make cloth as quickly and cheaply as the new looms. Their leaders urged "war against the machines — yes, 'war to the knife.'" Occasionally mobs rioted and wrecked the machines.

The 19th-century historian Edward Baines, however, argued in favor of the new inventions. A single 100-horsepower steam engine could power 50,000 spindles and produce 62,000 miles (100,000 kilometers) of thread in 12 hours — as much as 750 hand spinners could produce in a year. This, Baines wrote in 1835, "is the reason this industry can provide work and bread for a lot more people . . . and of such results we should not complain."

A weaver tries out one of the new flying shuttles, knocking it to and fro with a mechanism called a picker.
Below: *Legend says that James Hargreaves got the idea for his spinning jenny when he knocked over a spinning wheel. On its side the wheel can turn 16 spindles at once. A moving clamp is pulled away from the spindles to stretch the rovings into thread (left). Meanwhile, the spinner turns the wheel, which turns the spindles and twists the thread (center). When the "faller wire" is dropped onto the thread and the clamp moved back, the spun thread automatically winds onto the spindle (right).*

The First Factories

The early inventions used what is called intermediate technology; they were ingenious devices but could be made fairly easily. This encouraged industrialists to introduce them. Arkwright employed a local clockmaker to make the first spinning frame. Cartwright eventually remembered his first power loom with embarrassment: "The reed fell with the weight of at least half a hundredweight [100 pounds, or 45 kilograms] and the springs that threw the shuttle were strong enough to have powered a Congreve war rocket."

But even though the new machines were easy to make, they were too bulky to be used in people's homes and too heavy to be run by human effort. After 1781, when James Watt managed to turn the up-and-down movement of his steam engine into rotary (circular) movement, steam engines could be used to power the mules and looms. Such engines and machines had to be housed in factories. In 1771 Arkwright built a cotton factory in the village of Cromford in Derbyshire. Other industrialists soon followed his example. For the first time textile workers traveled from their homes to "go to work"—

a completely new idea for most people.

Minding the machines was desperately dull work, and at first people who were used to working at home or on the land resisted employment in the factories. To attract workers, Arkwright had to build houses, a church, and an inn for them. When anti-industry mobs threatened the mill, he collected 1,500 pistols, 500 spears, and a number of cannons to defend it.

At first Arkwright and other industrialists are eager to attract anyone who wants to work. But later it becomes hard for older men to get jobs in the mills. Women and children, who are easier to discipline and cheaper to employ than men, can join broken threads and sweep under equipment. In America women usually work for a third less wages than men.

A new concept of time has entered people's lives; they "clock on" and "clock off" at the factory and are paid according to the number of hours they work (instead of by the piece). As the overseer is often the only person with a watch, he decides when work starts and finishes; anyone coming late may be fined. A normal working day lasts from sunrise to sunset; in summer, workdays can be 14 or even 16 hours long. These workers are eating breakfast during their 15-minute break at 9:00 A.M. They have already done three hours' work.

Factory owners come to control their work forces completely. Arkwright's partner, Jedediah Strutt of Derbyshire, fines his young workers for even minor misbehavior such as "calling through the window to soldiers, riding on each other's backs, terrifying S. Pearson with an ugly face, and putting Josh Haynes's dog into a bucket of hot water."

Coal

The new factories created a tremendous demand for coal. A 40-horsepower Watt steam engine powering looms for 15 hours used 2 tons a day. Consequently, factories were often built near coalfields.

Changes in the iron industry also increased demand for coal. Since the Middle Ages iron had been produced by smelting (melting) the ore using charcoal (which is made from wood). A shortage of wood, however, led in the 1780s to Henry Cort's discovery of how to make wrought iron using coal. Air heated by the coal was passed over the iron while a workman "puddled" (stirred) the molten metal with a long pole.

As a result of these developments, the coal industry expanded. British coal output increased from 11 million tons in 1800 to nearly 34 million tons in 1840.

Despite this growth, the British coal industry did not introduce any major innovations down in the mines. The coal continued to be dug out with pickaxes by filthy, wet miners working in seams that were sometimes only 2 feet (0.6 meters) high. Mines increased their output simply by digging deeper, which heightened the danger for workers. On the Newcastle coalfield in the north of England, 1,468 miners died between 1799 and 1840. They were killed by explosions, suffocating chokedamp (carbon

monoxide), collapsing roofs, flooding, run-away trucks, and horrific falls.

In Britain, until the Mines Act of 1842, women and young girls, sometimes only 12 years old, drag tubs of coal from the seam to the mine shaft. Even younger children also work underground, minding the trapdoors that direct a flow of air through the tunnels. They sit in the dark, listening to rats scurrying and layers of rock settling. "It does not tire me, but I have to trap without a light and I'm scared — sometimes I sing," confesses Sarah Gooder, aged eight. The Mine Act of 1842 will forbid humans to drag the tubs of coal, and engines or ponies will take over. **Right:** *Most deaths in British mines occur from explosions caused by firedamp (methane gas). This builds up in areas of the mine that have not been properly ventilated, perhaps because a "trapper" has forgotten to close a trapdoor. The invention of the Davy safety lamp (1815) actually increases the number of deaths, because it allows "fiery" pits to be worked more extensively. Firedamp*

causes only a small explosion, but it whips into the air large amounts of coal dust, which — as a pocket of air surrounds each speck — is also explosive. A second, more destructive explosion follows.

The First Railways

The railroad grew out of the need to move heavy loads of coal. By 1700 many wagonways had been carved along the Newcastle coalfield. Ponies pulled wagonloads from the mines to the ships that carried the coal to London. As early as 1712 steam engines were used to drain the collieries and after the 1780s they were used to wind men up and down the shafts in "cages." Each colliery employed an "engine tenter" to look after the engines. These men began to experiment with moving steam engines, using the power of the engine to drive the wheels. In the early 1820s, businessmen in the Newcastle area hired George Stephenson, engine tenter at Killingworth Colliery, to build a railway between the Darlington coalfields and the port at Stockton.

The project was a success, but the railways faced opposition. Canal owners feared for their own livelihoods. Farmers claimed that the railways would destroy agriculture; cows would stop producing milk, hens would stop laying, and grass would wither and die, they said. Stephenson ignored all the criticism. Once a member of Parliament, wanting to prove the railways were unsafe, quizzed him: "Suppose . . . that a cow were to get in the way of the engine—

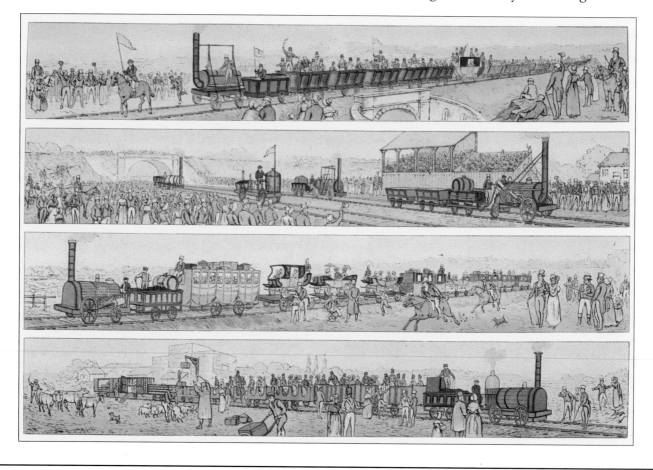

would that not be an awkward circumstance?" "Very awkward," Stephenson replied, "for the cow."

In 1826 Stephenson began to build the Liverpool to Manchester Railway; in 1833 it became the world's first passenger line operated solely by steam locomotives. The next year he began work on the London to Birmingham Railway; 112 miles (180 kilometers) long, it took 20,000 laborers four years to build and cost £5.5 million ($22 million). By 1840 Britain had 1,800 miles (3,000 kilometers) of railways, which had carried 18 million passengers during that year.

Right: *George Stephenson's engine the* **Locomotion.**

Left, above: *The Primrose Hill railway tunnel (1837).*

Left, below, top to bottom: *The* Locomotion *pulls the train on opening day of the Stockton and Darlington Railway (1825), the world's first steam-hauled public railway.*

The Rainhill locomotive trials (1829). Stephenson's engine, the Rocket, *wins the race, traveling at an average speed of 29 miles (47 kilometers) per hour.*

First-class carriages on the Liverpool to Manchester Railway (1833).

Second-class carriages also travel between Liverpool and Manchester.

Making Machines

As industry and transport adopted the new technology, there was a need for a new skill — engineering. In order to create and run railways, inventors like Stephenson needed rails, wagons, wheels, tubes, steam gauges, and turntables that could bear the stresses of accelerating and braking at speeds of up to 60 miles (97 kilometers) per hour. Companies such as the Whessoe Iron Foundry, which supplied the Stockton and Darlington Railway in England, met this new challenge.

A similar process was changing the cotton industry. As factories were built, firms were set up to make, install, and mend the machines. By 1839 one engineer, Charles Fairburn of Manchester, England — who had started in 1816 with a shed, a lathe, and "a strong Irishman to help" — employed 600 men in a large factory.

If the first stage of the Industrial Revolution was inventing machines to do the work of men, the next step was inventing machine tools — machines to make the machines. Engineers developed machines for boring (1774); making screws (1800); planing wood (1802); cutting gears (1820); grinding (1834); and shaping (1836). In the United States, Eli Whitney developed the idea of machines with interchangeable parts. Now industrialists could buy a part in quantity and use it for several kinds of machine. Because it greatly increased efficiency and made purchasing easier, this "American system" was soon introduced into Europe.

The foreman (center) is showing a group of journalists, including several foreign visitors, around this engineering workshop. The latest gear-cutting machinery in this well-run establishment will be the subject of newspaper articles that will interest many readers.

The Revolution Spreads

By 1800 British manufactured goods were flooding into European and American markets; because they had been machine made, their prices were low. In order to compete, European and American businessmen began to industrialize. A stream of entrepreneurs visited Britain, including the first French locomotive builder, Marc Séguin, who spent some time working for George Stephenson.

Many of these visitors were sent by their governments, which were becoming alarmed by Britain's growing power. Charles Dupin, a professor at the Conservatoire des Arts et Métiers in Paris, made six trips between 1818 and 1824, and he put together six enormous books full of detailed drawings of British technology. The government of Prussia, a northern German state, sent dozens of industrialists, industrial spies (some of whom lived permanently in London), civil servants, and even a lieutenant of artillery, Carl Wilhelm Bormann. But because these countries lacked the technological skills to use the machines they copied, many of their early attempts to acquire British know-how failed.

Meanwhile, British companies began to take precautions to keep possible spies and imitators out. They made their factories into fortresses with thick walls and small windows, and they required their workers to swear to keep their techniques secret. British authors describing those techniques left out important details so other industrialists at home and abroad would not be able to copy them completely. Not until the 1830s did the British relax their hold on these industrial secrets.

THE UNITED STATES

Until the end of the American Revolution (1775–1783), the 13 colonies, later states, in America belonged to Britain. They supplied Britain with raw materials in return for manufactured goods. Even after the war, British industrialists consciously tried to destroy American industry, to keep the United States their supplier country. But American businessmen like Eli Whitney contributed ideas and inventions to the Industrial Revolution from its beginning.

In addition, as the population of the United States grew — from 3.9 million in 1790 to 7.2 million in 1810 — American manufacturing developed to cater to this

growing market. As early as 1790 Samuel Slater had built the first American factory, a cotton mill in Rhode Island; many other factories soon followed.

Industrialization was welcome in the United States because it was seen as part of an exciting new way of life in a new world. Between 1820 and 1840, investment in American industry rose from $50 million to $250 million.

EUROPE

Unlike Americans, many European workers found it hard to adapt to industrialization. Adam Young, an English foreman in a French cotton mill, claimed in 1824 that "with one English worker I could have done more than I did with eight Frenchmen." One answer was to hire British workers and experts who would import their knowledge. In 1785 the French government employed the English ironmaster William Wilkinson to modernize their ironworks at

Le Creusot; in the early years of the 19th century half its 600 workers were British.

After Britain, Belgium was the first European country to industrialize successfully. Steam engines were introduced into Belgian mines in 1720. The textile industry prospered between 1806 and 1814, when Napoleon forbade imports of English cloth as part of his strategy to defeat Britain dur-

ing the Napoleonic Wars. The Belgian engineering industry exported machines to the rest of Europe, and Belgian mechanics (like English workmen) were employed in German and Austrian factories.

The German states also began to industrialize in the early 19th century. Factories were already spinning cotton; the first mill, with a water-powered Arkwright frame, was built in 1794 at Kromford, near Düsseldorf. After 1818 the German states began to form a *Zollverein* (free-trade union); by 1834 most of the German states belonged to it. In the same year Alfred Krupp converted his iron foundry in the Ruhr from water power to steam.

In France businessmen were cautious, but growth was still steady. A textile industry grew up on the coalfields of the northeast, and iron was made in Alsace-Lorraine. By 1841 an English visitor declared that the French engineers were as good as the Belgians, and that their machines looked better.

Though the spread of the Industrial Revolution brought new prosperity to some people, it limited the futures of others. More money was required to start a factory than to set up a shop or domestic manufacture, so most skilled workers discovered that they would never be able to have their own businesses. It was also difficult to advance through the ranks of employees; employers kept costs down by staffing their factories with more apprentices (people just learning their trade) than journeymen (skilled workers).

Far left: *In 1851 the London Society of Arts organizes the Great Exhibition in the Crystal Palace in Hyde Park. Officially called the Exposition of the Industry of All Nations, the exhibition includes machine tools for planing, drilling, and boring made at Joseph Whitworth's engineering factory in Manchester. Six million people come to wonder at the marvels of industry and technology. Two years later a similar exhibition is held in New York.* **Above left:** *The Forge Anglaise (English forge) at Le Creusot, built in 1827.*

Factory Work

Wherever the new factory system was introduced, debate followed. Children were an important part of the work force; they had small, quick hands and

could be paid less than adults. When Samuel Slater's mill opened in Rhode Island, the oldest worker was only 12. Many people felt it was wrong to introduce children into the "morally dangerous" world of industry. Others, like the English writer Andrew Ure, felt that, even for children, work such as tying threads was not hard: "It was delightful . . . to see them at leisure after a few seconds' exercise of their tiny fingers."

Most 19th-century factories, however, were grim, brutal places, and workers' conditions were harsh. In 1835 the French writer L. R. Villermé watched workers in Nantes walking to the factory — a journey that added an hour each way to their daily shift of 14 or 15 hours. "It is worth recalling that legislation fixes the working day even

for convicts at 12 hours," he observed.

Cotton factories had to be kept hot and wet to stop the threads from snapping, so textile workers who had to walk home through the cold night air tended to catch pneumonia. They also suffered from a respiratory disease called byssinosis, caused by cotton dust. None of the machines had safety guards, so accidents were common among the ragged, long-haired workers, especially the young "scavengers" who swept the waste from under the machines.

Children who had to stand all day suffered from knock knees or bow legs. Beatings and accidents increased toward the end of the long working day. Punishments included being beaten with a strap or thrown into tubs of water. In one British workshop a boy who worked too slowly had his ear nailed to the bench.

Although conditions improve as the century progresses, factories continue to introduce larger, faster machines that make the work even more demanding, while wages (being handed out by a clerk, above left) remain low. One female cotton worker complains that, although the working day has been reduced to ten hours, she works "as if the Devel was after us . . . what with the heat and the hard work . . . we are tould to Be content in the station of Life to wich the Lord as places us But I say the Lord never Did place us there so we have no Right to be content." Left: The mill office from which the manager (seen above on the factory floor) maintains strict discipline. In one cotton mill office in Lancashire, England, the manager requires his clerks to work in silence from 7:00 A.M. until 6:00 P.M. They each have to bring four pounds (two kilograms) of coal a day for the stove. "Calls of nature are permitted and the staff may use the garden below the second gate."

Life in the Cities

The population of industrial towns grew rapidly, partly because of the steady migration of people from the countryside. The centers of these towns reflected the wealth that industrialization had created; they had well-paved roads, magnificent town halls, luxurious stores, and fine statues financed by public subscription.

This, however, was the age of "two nations," or two very different ways of life. Away from the attractive main streets and the suburbs where the wealthy lived lay blackened factories, slag heaps, open sewers, and hundreds of cramped courts (alleys) where most people lived in overcrowded, badly built houses. In 1835 a Frenchman, Dr. Ange Guépin, described the houses in the rue des Fumiers in Nantes: "Go in, if the fetid smell which attacks you does not drive you back. . . . You will see two or three rickety beds with worm-eaten legs, a mattress, a tattered blanket of rags . . ."

Workers crowded together to save rent. As late as 1893, a German textile worker described a house in Berlin: In the attic the

landlady slept with her 14-year-old son on a straw mattress; her niece shared the back room with a 60-year-old man and a 15-year-old laundress; in the front room, the landlady's brother slept on the sofa, and her nephew (who paid extra to keep his suitcase in the room) had a hammock. On Sundays the front room was let out to a professional fortune-teller.

Nineteenth-century town governments did not create these slums on purpose; the swelling populations were simply overwhelming. Bradford in England was the center of the world's wool industry. Its population in 1780 was about 8,700. By 1841, with a population of 66,718, it had outgrown its sewage system to such an extent that in certain places the canal water was almost solid with human excrement and industrial waste. So many "offensive gases" were produced that in hot weather the water, from which many people had to drink, sometimes caught fire.

Polluted drinking water caused epidemics of dysentery, typhoid, and cholera (which swept Europe and America several times between 1817 and 1899). In cold, damp rooms everywhere, medical complaints such as rheumatism, bronchitis, anemia, rickets, and tuberculosis were all too common. Neither employers nor the state paid workers when they were sick, so illness forced families to give up even cheap lodgings. In Boston it was estimated that an Irish immigrant could expect to work 14 years before poor conditions led to death.

Life in the cities is hard. City governments slowly introduce improvements such as gas lighting (right), sewers, and water mains.
Left: Overcrowding is one of the primary problems faced by cities.
Above left: In 1851 there are still few sewers in London. Nightmen clean out cesspits where human excrement from the neighborhoods' privies (latrines) has collected. This produces such an appalling smell that the laborers are forbidden to work by day.

The Railways Expand

Railway "mania" swept the world. By 1900 there were nearly 200,000 miles (320,000 kilometers) of track in the United States, including four transcontinental lines. An extensive rail system helped settle America, moving people, animals, and goods at astonishing speeds; it effectively unified the country and was crucial to the development of trade. The gold spike that was used to connect the first transcontinental railroad at Promontory Point, Utah Territory, on May 10, 1869, was inscribed: "May God continue the unity of our Country, as this Railroad unites the two great Oceans of the World."

Railroads made the Great Plains available for farming and linked the industry of the East with the gold mines of California, the cattle ranches of Texas, and the coal mines of Pennsylvania. Railroads, natural resources, and a booming population enabled the United States economy to grow faster than that of any other country.

In 1910 the European network comprised 170,000 miles (275,000 kilometers) of track. Six years earlier, even comparatively backward Russia had completed a trans-Siberian railway from Moscow to Vladivostok. This was Russia's second attempt; initially the track had been laid in winter across the ice of Lake Baikal, and in spring a train had crashed through the ice and been lost.

Railroads eventually were built in Africa, Australia, India, and South America. Around the world the railways stimulated the coal and iron industries and created jobs for thousands of workers. Freight costs fell, reducing the prices of goods that trains moved. Transport became faster; fresh food, notably milk and meat, could be brought into the cities, improving the health of the middle and upper classes.

Communications also got better; the postal services used the railways, and the telegraph was developed to improve communication between stations in order to increase safety.

The railroads also changed how people thought about time. For centuries each town or city had had its own time, determined by the position of the sun. In 1870 a passenger traveling from Washington, D.C., to San Francisco and trying to keep up with local time at each stop would have had to change his or her watch 200 times. This made scheduling trains difficult, and confusion sometimes led to accidents. So in 1883 local times were abolished and America was divided into four standard time zones. The *Indianapolis Sentinel* noted, "The sun is no longer boss of the job. People, 55 million of them, must eat, sleep, and work as well as travel by railroad time."

All across the North American continent Irish, Italian,

Polish, and Chinese laborers lay tracks for the expanding railways. At times, teams lay as much as 10 miles (16 kilometers) of track a day.
Above: *Beginning in the early 1850s, inventors in New York City propose designs like this one for an elevated railway to help ease the city's traffic problems. After much discussion, the first elevated railway is built in New York in 1868.*

Iron and Steel

The railways stimulated industry in the principalities, duchies, and counties of Germany more than anywhere else in Europe. In 1851, 90 percent of German iron was still made using charcoal, and German delegates at the Great Exhibition in London believed that "Germany will never reach the level of coal and iron currently produced in England. We do not have the resources."

In the 20 years after 1850, however, nearly 9,000 miles (14,500 kilometers) of railway were built in Germany. Seventy-five new companies were set up to make the iron for the rails, trains, and rolling stock. Some of the companies were huge — the Hörder Verein works in the Ruhr employed 1,700 workers. Business boomed. In one year alone Krupp added 300 iron-ore mines, two foundries, and a fleet of ships to his industrial empire. All the new foundries used coal to smelt the iron, so by 1870 coal output had increased 600 percent. Germany was producing almost twice as much coal as France.

At the same time, German engineering was developing. At the Paris Exhibition of 1867, visitors marveled at Hörder Verein steel plates and at German military armaments such as a 50-ton Krupp cannon that fired shells weighing 1,000 pounds (450 kilograms). Four years later troops from the German state of Prussia took advantage of Germany's growing industrial strength; they went to war with France, destroyed the French army, and proclaimed a united German empire.

The German economy was growing by 10 percent per year, a rate matched only by the United States. Otto von Bismarck, the German chancellor, preached "blood and iron" (referring to war), but Germany's newfound unity and power, commented the economist J. M. Keynes, "was built more truly on coal and iron" (industrial strength).

A worker pours iron, smelted in a furnace, into a mold. Cast iron is cheaply and easily produced. It is used for a whole range of items, from fire engines to fireplaces (above).

Left: *The open-hearth furnace at the Llanelly steel works in Wales. Steel is a form of iron that has been hardened by being heated with carbon and then suddenly cooled. It is much stronger than cast iron and more malleable (able to be molded) than wrought iron. It is, however, much more expensive to produce until, in 1856, Henry Bessemer discovers a cheap way of making steel, using what will be called the Bessemer converter.*

Krupp's representative in London is a friend of Bessemer, and before long Krupp is producing steel to make weapons. Most German firms, however, do not adopt the converter so quickly. Their reluctance works to their advantage, because after 1878 they are able to introduce an even better method called the Gilchrist-Thomas process.

Bridges, Tunnels, and Towers

Railway building created dramatic new challenges for engineers; they had to find ways to tunnel through mountains and cross marshes and rivers. In 1825 the engineers of the world's first railway bridge used four spans (spaces between supports) to cross a stream only 24 feet (7 meters) wide. Fifty years later, in St. Louis, Missouri, James Eads completed a steel-arch bridge that crossed the 500 feet (152 meters) of the Mississippi in just three spans.

In 1889 in Paris, Alexandre-Gustave Eiffel built a tower of steel 984 feet (300 meters) high and weighing 18,000 tons, using 12,000 struts and 2,500,000 rivets. He intended the now famous tower to show the strength of steel, which it did.

American architects were using steel frames for all large buildings, attaching the walls to the frames. Using the new hydraulic lift (1857), builders were able to transport materials to great heights, as they built their "skyscrapers." This method of building around frames was called Chicago construction, because the first skyscraper was the ten-story Home Insurance building in Chicago, Illinois (1883–1885). The same principle was applied to ordinary housing, using wood and nails instead of steel girders and rivets; this technique was called balloon construction. It enabled builders to erect new houses much more quickly, and it did a great deal to lessen the misery of the early industrial towns.

Paralyzed and ill after repeated cases of the bends, Washington Roebling, chief engineer of New York's Brooklyn Bridge, oversees the construction from his home. His instructions are passed to the workmen by his wife, Emily, who in 1883 will be the first person to cross the bridge.

The Money Men

The need to raise large amounts of money for building railways, bridges, and factories led to the growth of stock exchanges where "shares" in companies (called joint stock companies) were sold to the public. Ordinary people invested their money both at home and abroad through the stock exchanges; the Brooklyn Bridge, for example, cost investors a total of $9 million. Through stock exchanges the savings of millions of people financed economic growth all over the world.

Many joint stock companies, however, went bankrupt, ruining thousands of small investors. Some directors did not hesitate to use other people's money to make themselves wealthy. Others, such as the American financier Jay Gould, "played the stock market." He called his method "profit through destruction," and his treatment of the Union Pacific Railway Company shows how it worked. In 1873 Gould published articles in his newspaper, the *New York World*, undermining confidence in the company. When the price of its shares collapsed, Gould bought a majority holding. Having gained control of the company, he made it buy, at a very high price, two railways he owned. Then his newspaper praised the Union Pacific until the price of its shares rose, and finally, in 1879, he sold most of his shares, claiming to have done the public a great favor by returning so valuable a company to thousands of "widows, orphans, and lady stockholders."

A widow and a laborer, each with a little money to spare, make deposits at a savings bank. The bank will invest the money and pay them interest. At the same time, angry creditors try to get into the bank to withdraw their funds — they have heard that the bank has invested in a business venture that is about to fail. Banks are notoriously unstable and many do go bankrupt.

The Second Revolution

T he inventions of the early Industrial Revolution came from the minds of ingenious mechanics, not scientists. After 1850, however, there was a much greater emphasis on science, as engineers explored ways of using new scientific knowledge for industry. Historians have called this period of applied science the second Industrial Revolution — a revolution based on gas, oil, electricity, and chemical engineering.

INDUSTRIAL CHANGE

Chemistry was crucial to the second revolution. In 1774 chemists had learned how to isolate oxygen and chlorine; now chlorine went into use as a bleach. Chloroform was used as an anesthetic, iodine as an antiseptic. In 1791 scientists had developed a process for obtaining alkali, which in the 19th century became a part of the soap-making process. In 1859 the first synthetic dye, magenta, was produced from coal tar, and other synthetic dyes soon went into making cloth. In 1860 an international chemical congress standardized names and symbols for many of the elements. Nine years later Russian Dimitri Ivanovich Mendeleyev and German Julius Meyer began to develop a standardized periodic table of the elements.

Coal gas, first extracted from burning coal in 1784, had been used on a small scale for lighting and heating since the early years

of the 19th century. In the century's second half its uses expanded; now many people used coal gas to heat and light their homes, and for cooking. Many towns began introducing gas lighting in public areas after dark to reduce crime and make their streets safer. A German engineer, Nicholas Otto, built an efficient four-stroke gas engine in 1876 and sold 30,000 of them in ten years. There was a boom in investment in gasworks between 1865 and 1885.

Another new fuel, petroleum, started to become available in the United States after the discovery of the Pennsylvania oilfields in 1859. It became vitally important for lighting and for lubrication; and gasoline (refined petroleum) was sold as a medicine. By 1917 nearly half a million oil wells had been sunk in America.

Meanwhile, electrical engineers were finding practical uses for electricity. In 1872 the Belgian engineer Zenobe Gramme invented an effective electric generator. In 1874 the electric trolley was innovated in America. Scientists developed new and increasingly efficient methods of communication that relied on electrical impulses — the electric telegraph, for example, in 1837. In 1876 American Alexander Graham Bell patented the telephone and Thomas Edison invented the gramophone. German physicist Heinrich Hertz discovered radio waves in 1883, and a working radio was innovated in 1896.

Electricity was increasingly used for lighting because it was cleaner and less dangerous than gas or oil. Thomas Edison invented a working light bulb in 1879. By 1882, the year when central generating stations opened in New York (Pearl Street), and London (Holborn), he had installed over 150 electrical generators in houses, hotels, mills, and ships.

Some new scientific theories and discoveries also began to challenge established explanations about how the world worked, and to raise new questions. In 1859 the English naturalist Charles Darwin published a book called *The Origin of Species by Natural Selection*. Darwin argued that living creatures had developed through a process of evolution whereby those species most "fitted" to their environment survived and prospered. The theory aroused a massive controversy throughout Europe and America, because it was used to attack the tradi-

tional story of Creation given in the Bible. The vice-chancellor of Cambridge University continued to assert that God had created the world at 9:00 A.M. on Monday, October 23, 4004 B.C., and in the United States John Scopes, a high school science teacher, was taken to court for teaching Darwin's theory.

Left: *The transmitter from which the first British radio broadcast (a news bulletin) was made in 1922.*
Above left: *Thomas Edison in his laboratory.*
Above: *Guglielmo Marconi, the inventor of the wireless telegraph.*

Reaching for New Markets

As their businesses expanded and their populations grew, European and American leaders constantly looked for new markets in which to sell their products, and for new sources of agricultural goods and raw materials. The British, for example, imported wheat from Argentina, Australia, India, America, Russia, and Canada. And the inventions of tin cans and refrigeration allowed ships to carry even perishable produce and meat all over the world.

Not all countries wanted to trade with the industrialized West. But the Western nations had mechanized warfare as well as industry, and their new war machines — particularly the gunboat and the machine gun — gave them a military advantage. Britain was the country most prepared to bully less powerful nations; in December 1838, when the Chinese government seized 20,291 chests of the illegal drug opium from

British traders, the British government sent in its navy. The Chinese were forced to "lease" Hong Kong to Britain in 1842 and to allow the British to trade in China freely.

America turned its eyes south and west to Native American and Spanish-held land. Invoking the idea of "Manifest Destiny" — meaning it was the United States's divinely decreed fate to rule the North American continent — the nation expanded aggressively, annexing Texas in 1845 and Oregon in 1846. A war with Mexico (1846–1848) added California, New Mexico, Nevada, Utah, and Arizona in 1848. Alaska was purchased from Russia in 1867. Troops crushed those people, such as Native Americans and Mormons, who resisted U.S. rule.

A steamship coming from the Far East travels down the Suez Canal. Built with a combination of British and French capital and opened in 1869, the canal shortens the journey between India and western Europe by 4,000 miles (6,400 kilometers). In 1875 the British government will buy a controlling interest in the canal. This action will spark off a scramble for colonies in Africa.

The Scramble for Empire

In the second half of the 19th century, the Industrial Revolution spread out from the countries of western Europe and the United States. Germans set up businesses in Austria-Hungary, the Balkans, and Turkey; they began planning a railway from Berlin to Baghdad in 1888. French banks funded Russian industry, shipyards, and banks. The United States invested millions of dollars in Cuba and Mexico.

Some countries managed to have their own industrial revolutions. Sweden used her vast resources of wood and iron to become an industrial power; Switzerland concentrated on highly priced, high-quality products; and Denmark, without coal or iron, used the new technologies to achieve an agricultural revolution.

Most nonindustrialized countries remained at the mercy of Western businessmen. Technology had advanced so far that these countries could not afford the vast outlay on machines, factories, transport, and communications that would be necessary if they were to compete. They continued to buy manufactured goods from the West and pay for them by supplying large amounts of raw materials cheaply. Thus, industrialized countries came to dominate the rest of the world economically.

IMPERIALISM

As the century progressed, competition between the industrialized nations became increasingly fierce. The United States and Germany began to move ahead of Britain in the race to become the world's leading industrial nation. But Britain did not want to lose her position as "workshop of the world."

The answer, it seemed, was not only to find new markets but also to close them to competitors. The best way to do this was to establish an empire, to conquer less developed countries and make them into colonies. There was also a growing jingoism in the industrialized nations — a feeling that they were superior to other nations — and it often mixed with racism. The English poet Rudyard Kipling urged his readers to take up the "white man's burden" to "civilize" the rest of the world.

Starting in the 1830s the French government openly tried to "revive the Roman Empire" in Africa; in Asia between 1862 and 1867 it won control of the lands known as Indochina. Between 1871 and 1900 Britain added 4.25 million square miles (11 mil-

lion square kilometers) and 66 million people to its empire. The British imperialist (empire builder) Cecil Rhodes even considered leaving money in his will to finance the reconquest of America. During 1884 and 1885 Germany gained 350,000 square miles (905,000 square kilometers) of territory in Tanganyika in east Africa. In 1885 King Leopold of Belgium acquired almost a mil-

lion square miles in the Congo; he then granted a series of monopolies that ensured that only Belgian companies could trade there.

To increase trade, the United States conquered the Spanish colonies of Puerto Rico and the Philippines, and annexed Hawaii (1898), adding those lands to the territory acquired from Mexico; it also established "protectorates" (actually, U.S.-run governments) over Cuba and Panama.

When they had conquered an area, the imperialist powers immediately opened it up for trade. Of prime importance were means of moving goods. The British built a railway from Cairo in Egypt to Cape Town in South Africa and stretched thousands of miles of track across India and Australia. The French planned a trans-Saharan railroad. In 1904, having already completed a transcontinental railroad at home, the United States began constructing the Panama Canal in Central America. When the canal was completed in 1914, ships traveling from the Atlantic to the Pacific no longer had to sail around South America.

Imperialism always gave the economic advantage to the conquerors. The new railroads, canals, and treaties allowed the industrial centers of the United States and western Europe to take wool from Australia, gold from Alaska, diamonds from South Africa, rubber from Malaysia, tea from India, and corned beef from Argentina all the more easily. The whole world had been mobilized to supply the industrial countries and to buy their manufactured goods.

Members of the Katenu tribe of Nigeria with an official of the British Royal Niger Company in 1883. In two years the British government will declare the area a "protectorate."
Above left: *British imperialists enjoy many luxuries in India.*
Left: *A local Muslim army and a British force, each seeking control of the Sudan, confront each other at the Battle of Omdurman (1898).*

41

Dreams and Realities

Between 1871 and 1911, approximately 28 million people left Europe. Of these, 20.5 million headed for America, the "Land of Opportunity"; the rest traveled to Europe's new colonies. The United States government, eager to fill new territories and new factories, welcomed immigrants; in 1907 more than one million passed through New York City's Ellis Island, the East Coast's main point for immigration.

Most immigrants were poor or working class people trying to make a better life, though a few were bankrupt businessmen, impoverished nobles, or criminals on the run. Some had their passage paid by their trade unions because their union activities had led to them being blacklisted at home. All hoped for a new start. Irish peasants escaped from starvation and poverty; Slovaks fled from political oppression in Hungary. From Russia came thousands of Jews, "pathetic with the silent story of persecution." Swedish and German farmers, often responding to advertisements in their newspapers, sold their farms at home and bought land from the American railroad companies — at $1.25 an acre. Italian peasants sold their houses to work as unskilled laborers in America. Gangs of Polish men were contracted to work on the railways; they traveled in groups of ten, each gang taking a woman to cook and wash for it. America also brought men from China to mine and to build railroads, but for a time the government forbade them to marry in the United States or to bring wives from home. Some English farmers traveled to America, but many more went to Australia or New Zealand seeking good pastureland.

Economic opportunities usually did improve for the immigrants. Most worked hard, and their children benefited from their efforts. Often an immigrant would work until he could pay for members of his family to come and join him, or he would send money home to support relatives. Still, many found the cultures to which they had been transplanted strange or even hostile. Joining society at the bottom and despised as "micks," "wops," "spics," "polacks," and "chinks," people from the same country clung together in neighborhoods and towns, almost always marrying only into families from the same ethnic background. Many became more fiercely nationalistic then ever, loving and longing for their home country.

These immigrants are traveling in steerage (the cheapest accommodation). They face a difficult and sometimes dangerous passage. There is a tub of herring in the hold, but often passengers are too seasick to eat. Fresh drinking water is usually only available up on deck. One man has died on this journey. The other passengers watch as his wife prepares to bury him at sea.

Above: *Dancing with joy as they enter New York harbor, these immigrants are eager to begin their new lives. They must still undergo medical examinations and legal interrogations on Ellis Island, though, before they will be allowed to meet their relatives or continue their journey to their new home in America. Each steerage passenger will be briefly examined by a doctor. If the passenger looks at all ill, the doctor will mark him or her with white chalk and he or she will be held for further examination. There is a hospital on Ellis Island where doctors can treat passengers, but passengers who have incurable diseases are sent back to the countries from which they came. Passengers who are not detained by the doctors move on to the immigration inspectors, who ask questions about marital status, skills, and prospective employment.*

Wealth

The Industrial Revolution created great wealth — for some people. Alfred Krupp became the richest man in Germany, thanks largely to his special steel cannons, which set the standard in Western warfare. American businessman J. P. Morgan left $80 million when he died. For some, this new wealth became a means of entry to the upper classes; the daughter of American industrialist Henry Singer (of Singer sewing machines) married the Prince de Polignac.

In addition to these very wealthy people, there was a growing middle class. Some scholars of the time divided this group into "upper middle class" (industrialists, bankers, lawyers, and doctors) and "lower middle class" (shopkeepers, craftsmen, teachers, civil servants, and clerks). In some respects the 19th-century middle-class lifestyle still influences the popular stereotype of what constitutes a "happy family."

Most middle-class families aspired to live in a detached house with a garden. In Boston, a father advised his son: "When you marry, pick out a suburb to build a house in, join the Country Club, and make your life center about your club, your home, and

your children." The family of the British economist J. M. Keynes was typically upper middle class; the Keyneses employed three servants and a governess and took two holidays a year, including a month in Switzerland. Many middle-class families were religious, and the day usually began with the whole household, including the servants, praying together. Moral correctness was considered vital.

While the successful middle-class man went to work in his office, his wife ran the household, dealt with the tradesmen, and organized the servants who looked after the children and did the housework. Occasion-ally, she might venture out in a horse-drawn cab to one of the new department stores. Although legally under her husband's control, she would probably look on the idea of women's suffrage (women voting in elections) with horror. Some unmarried girls and women went to work in offices, often operating typewriters (invented in 1868).

This late 19th-century German dollhouse shows a typical wealthy middle-class household. The family lives upstairs in luxury. Servants are an essential mark of the family's wealth, but they work mainly downstairs in the kitchen. On the top floor are the children's nursery and the servants' sleeping quarters.

Philanthropy

The early Industrial Revolution idealized the self-made man. Many people believed that poverty was the result of idleness, drunkenness, or low morals. Most industrialists opposed government intervention in business, believing they should be allowed to run their companies on their own terms. They kept wages as low as possible and got as much work out of their employees as they could, claiming that a hard worker could become a millionaire.

By the end of the century many middle-class individuals and organizations felt intervention to improve the living and working standards of the poor was necessary. In the United States child-labor committees, church organizations, and women's clubs campaigned to improve conditions by changing the law. In 1880 only seven states regulated children's labor; by 1900 most states had laws forbidding factories to employ children at "dangerous" tasks. Philanthropists also worked to establish libraries, parks, and playgrounds. As landscape architect Frederick Law Olmstead said of New York's Central Park, these places for clean, moral recreation had "a distinctly harmonizing and refining influence on the most unfortunate classes of the city."

Women, who were becoming more and more interested in politics, often took the lead in philanthropic campaigns. In the 1840s Sarah Bagley fought to get women's workday limited by law to ten hours; Jane Addams started Hull House in Chicago in

land large firms such as Krupp (armaments), Bayer (chemicals), and Suchard (chocolate) built "model villages" with good housing and amenities for their workers. Starting in 1896 the German textile firm of Peters and Company operated a welfare plan that included a sickness fund, a savings bank, a pension fund, help with house purchasing, a welfare institute for lectures and social events, public baths and showers, a steam laundry, and a library.

1889, offering an education and help for immigrants adapting to American culture.

Some industrialists were true philanthropists, helping to improve their workers' lives. In 1867 the manager of the Krenholm cotton factory in Narva, Russia, started a movement to reduce the hours a child might work each day. In Germany and Switzer-

Children prepare for dinner in a London orphanage in 1901. Conditions have improved greatly since the early 19th century, when the principle of English poor relief was that it must be so awful that it would be claimed only by those who were desperately in need.
Above left: *During the 19th century many towns open public libraries. Here, workers in Manchester, England, read the latest news from America.*

Unions, Politics, and Laws

After 1850 many workers joined trade or labor unions and organized themselves to fight for regular hours, better pay, protection for child laborers, and healthier working environments. In Britain the first Trades Union Congress was held in 1868; by 1912 — a year in which 40 million working days were lost in strikes — there were 3.4 million trade unionists in Britain. Also in 1912, the German Trades Union Congress (formed in 1892) had 2.5 million members. In the United States, membership of the American Federation of Labor grew fivefold between 1898 and 1904, when it reached 1.7 million. In 1917 AFL membership had reached 2.4 million, while the competing Industrial Workers of the World union (whose members were known as Wobblies) claimed an additional 60,000 to 100,000 American members.

Labor unions did well during times of prosperity, when employers were prepared to meet the workers' demands. In times of depression, however, employers refused to give way. Many workers turned from the unions, accepting half-time jobs or cut wages, just so they could keep earning something. Others started to become involved in politics instead.

SOCIALISM

In 1848 Karl Marx, a German professor, worked with Friedrich Engels, the son of a

factory owner, to write and publish a pamphlet titled *The Communist Manifesto*. In it they claimed that the workers of the world had become "wage slaves" of the middle class, who not only owned business but dominated government. They urged the working classes to unite to overthrow the middle class — either by revolution or by winning an election in those countries (such as America) where workingmen had the vote.

The general movement with which Marx and Engels were involved was called socialism. Socialists believed that the state or the community, not individual industrialists, should own the factories and tools that produced the wealth. In America between 1868 and 1885 several cooperative factories were founded, owned by the people who worked in them.

Though socialism was not popular among the ruling classes and many people tried to stamp it out, a number of working-class socialist parties were formed. In 1889 the Second International Working Men's Association met in Paris, with members from all over Europe and the United States, and even one from Japan. A socialist party was formed in France in 1905 and one year later the Labour party took shape in Britain.

In the Swedish parliamentary elections of 1907, Social Democrats won 64 seats out of 230. The Socialist Party of America (formed in 1901 from two smaller groups) reached its greatest strength in 1912 when Eugene Debs, the Socialist candidate for president, received nearly a million votes. The same year the German Social Democratic party (founded in 1875) had 4 million supporters and was the largest party in the German *Reichstag* (parliament).

LAWS

Organized into strong unions and large political parties, workers were able to campaign for changes in the law. To try to prevent the whole working class from becoming socialist, governments adopted legislation that would benefit laborers. The German government introduced health insurance (1883) and old-age pensions (1889) specifically to "check the spread of socialism" and prevent a revolution. In Britain the Third Reform Act (1884) gave the vote to all men over the age of 21, and by 1914 the government had introduced unemployment benefits, national health insurance, and old-age pensions. The French government regulated hours of work (1892), provided for free medical treatment (1893), and introduced child allowances (1913).

In the years after 1903, American states enacted laws restricting the number of hours children and women could work, setting minimum wages for women, and establishing workers' compensation for on-the-job injuries. Some groups also tried to get jobs away from immigrants and give them to native-born workers. The Workingmen's

Party of California, for example, pressured the American government to prevent the Chinese from coming over to work on the railways; they succeeded in 1882, when a law was enacted preventing Chinese immigration for the next ten years.

Certain workers slowly began to benefit from the Industrial Revolution. Real wages (money wages, taking account of the changes in prices) increased by over 50 percent in Britain and Germany between 1850 and 1914. Increased sales of goods such as sugar and meat also indicated gradually increasing wealth. Nevertheless, there was still great financial inequality between the rich and the poor. According to a survey of 1906, for example, 0.5 percent of the population of Great Britain owned 33 percent of the nation's wealth.

Striking iron workers march for higher wages.
Left: *The union leader Mary MacArthur speaks to box-makers in London in 1908.*

Education

Gradually, governments were making certain changes to improve people's lives; change happened first where not only the workers but also the government and industrialists could hope to benefit. Education was one such area.

Officials believed that education's purpose was to improve the morals of the downtrodden and to teach them the discipline useful in factory work or the military. In 1877 the American commissioner of education hoped that "schools could train the children to resist the evils of strikes and violence." In Germany a royal command of 1889 instructed teachers to make sure their students understood that "the working classes can trust only the Kaiser [emperor] for justice and the safety of their wages."

Schools for the workers' children were often structured like factories; whereas students of all levels used to learn in one large room, many towns started to divide them into numbered grades. When this was done in the early 1870s in Lynn, Massachusetts, the school board announced the change by comparing the new system to an efficient assembly line, in which tasks were specified and one job thoroughly done before the product (the student!) moved on to the next level.

Between 1870 and 1914 some form of education was made compulsory in most of Europe and the United States; state governments gradually took over responsibility for running schools, financing them with tax money. The number of primary-school teachers trebled in Sweden; in Finland the number of children in primary schools increased thirteenfold. German schools, which put great emphasis on practical, technical, and scientific subjects, were said to be far ahead of any other country's.

For wealthy young men universities offered not only higher education but also enormous opportunities to meet people and form what would become business relationships. During college or upon graduating, a young man could join a fraternity and mix with people from his own background. There were a number of colleges for young women as well, and late in the century, a very few young women also started attending universities.

This class of young German pupils has just finished an algebra lesson. Now they have opened their history books. Much of their work consists of memorizing long lists of facts.

Their teacher is a stern disciplinarian; punishments include flogging with the cane, shackling pupils to a desk, hanging logs around their necks, putting them in a basket hanging from the roof, and parading them around the school in a tin or paper hat.

Medicine and Health

Until about 1860, in the words of one nurse, hospitals did "more harm than good." Patients were crowded together in beds and frequently went unwashed until they died; hospital staff tried to avoid touching them whenever possible. Many patients died of blood poisoning after surgery. Before anesthetics were introduced, surgeons rushed through operations to limit the pain; British surgeon Robert Liston could amputate a leg in two and a half minutes.

Meanwhile, cholera epidemics (1817–1899) that spread from slums to the suburbs where wealthy people lived led to an outcry for something to be done about public health. Governments were alarmed because a large proportion of army volunteers were too sick or weakened by disease for military service. Industrialists hoped production would improve if fewer working days were lost through sickness.

In 1857 Louis Pasteur, a French chemist, offered a startling new theory: germs, invisible to the naked eye, cause disease. On the basis of this theory, governments began to introduce laws to improve public health and town planning. Germany led the way, with many towns adopting "municipal socialism," financing the building of sewers, gasworks, and waterworks. People began washing their bodies and their food regularly. By the end of the century, epidemics of diseases such as cholera and typhoid had become largely a thing of the past in the West.

Anesthetics — laughing gas (1800), ether (1842), and chloroform (1847) — and antiseptics improved patients' chances of surviving surgery. Doctors began wearing masks and gloves during operations, and the risk of infection decreased. Other inventions — for instance, aspirin, X rays, and the electrocardiograph (which records heartbeats) — improved medical care. In the years after 1854 a British woman, Florence Nightingale, reformed the nursing profession by showing that women made excellent nurses, even on the battlefield. She also established standards for hygiene in hospitals.

Doctors tried to understand and fight infectious diseases. During the 1870s a German medical officer named Robert Koch discovered how to use coal-tar dyes to color germs, thereby showing which germ caused which disease. In the 1880s Pasteur's team of French scientists discovered how to inoculate against diseases such as tuberculosis and diphtheria by injecting a weakened form of a disease to infect the body and cause it to build up its defenses.

Sewers and clean tap water; inoculation; going into a hospital and being cured — these things were virtually unknown before the Industrial Revolution. During the 19th century the discoveries were made that allowed them to become commonplace today.

An operation at Saint Thomas's Hospital, London, in 1862. Anesthetics make the operation painless. Surgeons disinfect their surgical instruments and drench themselves, their patients, and the operating theater in a fine spray of germ-killing carbolic acid.
Below: *Building a sewer in London in 1859. Sewers and clean water save many more lives than all the other improvements in medical care put together.*

Women at Work

"Thirty morning gowns; now that I call real happiness," commented the upper-class heroine of a British novel written in 1830. The daily activities of most wealthy women in the early 19th century consisted mainly of needlework, painting, playing the piano, and dressing for meals. In middle-class families (and in more and more working-class families that aspired to the middle class) daughters and wives stayed at home. These women were tied to the house and totally dependent on their fathers or husbands. Some were happy; others felt frustrated and unfulfilled: "Oh weary days — oh evenings that never seem to end — and for 20, 30 years more to do this," wrote Florence Nightingale, before an income of £500 ($2,000) a year from her father enabled her to leave home and become a nurse.

After 1870 the position of women slowly began to change. Even though birth control was frowned upon (when the English union leader Annie Besant supported it, the courts took away her children), women began to have fewer children. Wives, no longer continuously pregnant, were freed to do other things. Education laws ensured that all girls received some schooling; nonetheless, sometimes university-educated women were criticized.

Middle-class women started to leave the home in order to work again. Compulsory education opened up teaching as a possible career. Women also became typists and telephone operators. A very few became doctors, authors, and journalists. Women joined the new socialist parties, formed clubs, ran Christian missions in working class areas, and campaigned against "the demon drink." In the United States the General Federation of Women's Clubs fought for better living and working conditions.

Attitudes changed. In 1893 women won the vote in New Zealand. By 1915 women had the vote in Australia, Finland, Norway, Denmark, Iceland, and some American states. Although the issue of a woman's right to vote had been first debated in America when the constitution was drafted in 1787, it was not until August 26, 1920, that the nineteenth amendment to the constitution insured American women that right. Demonstrations, vandalism, hunger strikes — even prison terms — had all been part of the long struggle to win the vote.

At the same time, women were expressing their right to social freedom in various ways. Strong-willed Americans known as "titanesses" rebelled by going to nightclubs to dance. In England some women wore "bonnets, loud stockings, capes, crinolines, and ringlets straying over the shoulder," shocking their elders.

New technology speeds up many household chores. The flatiron is replaced by the electric iron (1909), needle and thread by the sewing machine (1851), and dustpan and brush by the vacuum cleaner (1903). Washing machines (1880s) replace the washboard, and gas cookers (1880) replace the kitchen range.
Below: *Women stop wearing whalebone corsets. Instead, they put on looser, simpler clothes that give them more freedom and allow them to take part in new sports like tennis and bicycle riding.*

Mass Appeal

Toward the end of the 19th century, fashionable young people wanted to be avant-garde (ahead of everyone else). Everything was "new" — the new woman, *art nouveau, Neue Zeit ("New Age,"* the title of a Marxist newspaper). Painters startled audiences by using new colors and techniques such as impressionism, which was meant to give viewers a feeling rather than offering them an exact reproduction of the subject. For wealthy people there were even new diseases, including "tennis elbow" and "bicycle face."

Improved communications had made the world a smaller place, and the middle and upper classes prided themselves on their cultural awareness and refinement. They attended plays by diverse writers such as Norway's Ibsen, Britain's Shaw, and Russia's Chekhov. There were crazes for folk music and dance from many countries; Spanish flamenco, Argentinian tango, and Negro blues were popular in both Europe and America. The new art of photography made it possible for people to see images of famous sites around the world even if they themselves were never able to travel.

Music was extremely popular. In Germany the number of theaters trebled between 1870 and 1896. Huge audiences in several countries came to listen to opera

stars such as the Italian great Caruso and Australian Dame Nellie Melba (so popular a dessert was named after her). The German composer Richard Wagner caught the feeling of German nationalism, while imperialistic British audiences attended the outdoor London Promenade Concerts to sing about the glory of their country.

As the sky darkens, a film director tries to shoot the final scene of his movie. Rain or darkness will mean the actors and crew must stop their work for the day. Since early movies have to be shot in daylight, sets like this one are built outside, often near water (which reflects additional light).

First seen publicly in 1895, movies attract audiences of 50 million a week in the United States by 1914. At first the movies are silent, but in the late 1920s sound will be added.

Above: *An advertisement encourages members of Britain's upper and middle classes to take their vacations abroad. Less wealthy people might take a train to the ocean.*

Big Business

During the 1860s the scholar Herbert Spencer applied Darwin's ideas about evolution to business, coining the phrase "the survival of the fittest." He argued that the most ruthless industrialists, like the fittest species, naturally rose to the top.

Spencer's philosophy was accepted enthusiastically in the United States, where it was used to justify cutthroat competition. John D. Rockefeller forced smaller companies to merge with his Standard Oil Company until, by 1879, he controlled 90 percent of the oil-refining industry. He built pipelines to avoid using the railroads. He used his own tankers, made his own barrels, and manufactured oil lamps. Then he bought out the retailers and sold the oil himself.

American management methods led the world; they turned the Industrial Revolution into big business. To motivate their work force, many American firms introduced personnel departments, canteens, social clubs, and profit sharing. Businessmen formed huge corporations and powerful cartels (groups of firms that cooperate to fix prices and destroy opposition).

"The young American appears to be continually possessed by a determination to become something 'big,'" wrote an English visitor to New York in 1882. To work your way from poverty to riches — like Rockefeller, Andrew Carnegie (steel), George Pullman (railways), or Jay Gould (finance) — was the "American dream."

American businessmen revolutionize production methods. At Henry Ford's factory his Model T Ford car is mass-produced on a moving assembly line, where a conveyor belt takes the product past workers who each perform one of the many small tasks required to build it. In 1914 Ford produces 248,000 cars costing as little as $490 each, and he makes a profit of over $30 million. The motorcar provides millions of people with a hitherto unknown freedom of travel.

Into the Future

To many people the 20th century has seemed a golden age of advance, a sequence of technological marvels including the Wright brothers' airplane flight (1903), the invention and patenting of synthetic plastic (1909), the first television broadcasts (1927–1928), the development of the modern digital computer (1940s) and microcomputers (1970s), the development of nuclear power (1956), the first successful heart transplant (1967), the first moon landing (1969), and the birth of the first test-tube baby (1978).

Yet the Industrial Revolution has also created problems that we have not yet been able to solve. Nuclear weapons, first developed and used in 1945, have given world leaders the power to destroy every living thing on earth dozens of times over.

Expanded industry itself has created a threat to our safety. In the book *Limits to Growth* (1972), researchers and writers at the Massachusetts Institute of Technology point to the problems of pollution, population explosion, and overuse of the world's natural resources; the book forecasts that if these problems are not addressed, the human life system will be destroyed during the 21st century.

The Industrial Revolution has also made some countries rich while leaving others poor. The United States, which contains only 6 percent of the world's population, uses 33 percent of its oil, 44 percent of its coal, and 63 percent of its gasoline.

Some countries such as Japan, Taiwan, and South Korea have achieved their own industrial revolutions and now compete with the nations of the West, but it is very difficult for a nonindustrial country to have such a revolution. Not only is the technological leap greater now than ever, but the industrialized countries are organized into economic communities that effectively exclude others. Concerns about pollution and overuse of resources also make the technological leap harder.

The challenge we face now is to turn our many inventions to the task of creating wealth that can be shared among all the world's countries without polluting or destroying the earth.

Putting the inventions of the Industrial Revolution to destructive ends: The armies of World War I use airplanes first for reconnaissance (below), and later as fighters and bombers. Nitrate of ammonia (a fertilizer) is used for explosive shells, chlorine (a disinfectant used in hospitals) for poisonous gas, and coal-tar dyes to color soldiers' uniforms. Railways allow troops to be moved quickly to the front, where they confront and kill one another.

How Do We Know?

On Wednesday, September 15, 1830, Fanny Kemble of England rode on the railway. She was 19 years old, and the experience thrilled her: "What with the sight and sound of these cheering crowds and the tremendous speed [10 miles, or 16 kilometers, per hour] my spirits rose to champagne height." Her mother, however, was "frightened to death."

How do we know? Because Miss Kemble wrote it all down in a letter. Reading that letter today, historians can learn about the opening day of the first passenger railway and the attitudes of those who were present. If they read on, they find out about the first railway accident.

Novels by writers such as Charles Dickens (1812–1870), Elizabeth Gaskell (1810–1865), and Émile Zola (1840–1902) also offer vivid details of the environment and attitudes of the time. Historians must, however, remember that novels are fictional — the stories they tell are imagined.

Some contemporary sources attempt to give fair, objective, and factual accounts. Edward Baines's *History of the Cotton Manufacture* (1835), for example, was carefully researched and is still a valuable source of information; in it Baines recorded an interview with Edmund Cartwright. Dr. Villermé and Dr. Guépin, who wrote about the lives of French factory workers, used government statistics but also visited and interviewed individuals.

The number of newspapers increased throughout the 19th century, and scholars can use these papers to learn what happened each day. Historians can also investigate the account books and correspondence books of individual companies. Many government documents have been preserved, and as a result historians can read a decree made by the German Kaiser in 1889 or flip through a circular a French education minister wrote in 1893. Every ten years since 1790, the American government has taken a census recording the name, age, marital status, position in the household, occupation, and place of birth of every person in the country. Britain started a census in 1851. British parliamentary commissions recorded the ignorance of workers in 1841 and the terror small children felt in the mines. U.S. special consular reports give vital information about immigration. In fact, so many government reports exist that a historian could not read all of them in a lifetime.

Photographs are another important historical source. In 1839 the French inventor Louis J. M. Daguerre developed a technique for making photographic images on specially treated, light-sensitive copper plates. These images were known as daguerreotypes, after their inventor. In 1841 an Englishman named Fox Talbot patented the calotype, another important forerunner of the modern photograph. After 1895 it was possible to take "moving pictures" (films) to record people's lives and achievements.

Meanwhile, monuments of the Industrial Revolution survive everywhere — from the Eiffel Tower in Paris to the Brooklyn Bridge in New York, to the countless railways, factories, and mills built throughout the world. Smaller relics of daily life can be seen in industrial museums, although historians must remember that some museums do not merely preserve the remains of the past but also try to reconstruct "life as it used to be." If this is the case, the reconstruction is an interpretation by a modern historian and may not be correct.

USING THE SOURCES

For a historian investigating the years before 1800, the problem is to piece together scraps of evidence to create a picture of what life was like. For a historian studying the years after 1800, problems arise because there are actually too many sources.

Historians have to generalize from a mass of information. This can be difficult where the sources disagree as violently as Dr. Villermé and Andrew Ure do about the experiences of factory children. The historian has to consult as many sources as possible and try to come to a fair conclusion.

Not all sources are equally reliable. We cannot know whether the characters in a novel are typical of their time or unusual, for example. And sometimes writers let their prejudices affect their comments — for instance, the German writer who thought the Poles were poor because they were lazy.

Even government sources are not always reliable. The British Commission of 1832 on factory conditions was led by Michael Sadler, a keen reformer. It intended to prove that conditions were terrible. One of the witnesses — quoted in many history books — was Samuel Coulson, a factory worker. He claimed that, for six weeks when the mill was busy, his small children worked 19 hours a day and had only 3 hours' sleep a night. Do you believe him?

Sometimes even well-meaning people altered evidence. A book published for the British Ladies Society in about 1835 included a picture of a cotton mill (above right, top). The artist who drew the pictures for *Michael Armstrong, Factory Boy* (1840) — a moralistic novel about a factory worker's life — based one of his illustrations (middle) on this picture. Twenty years later another artist, who was illustrating *White Slaves of England*, further changed the picture to show the need for factory reform (bottom). The historian has to decide which picture best illustrates conditions in the factories. How would you decide?

YOUR TASK

Nineteenth-century historians believed that if they found out all the facts, they would discover the truth about the past. Nowadays

most historians think that each new generation selects from and reinterprets the available facts and develops new theories about what happened. Perhaps you will be one of the next generation of scholars who will have new ideas about the Industrial Revolution.

Start now. Choose any page of this book and ask in your local or school library for books of primary sources (sources from the time) about that topic. Read the sources and use them to criticize the statements in this book. Who says every conclusion in this book is correct?

Index

FIRSTS

• 1790 First American cotton mill, Rhode Island

• 1825 The Stockton

• 1830 *Tom Thum*

• 1712 First steam engine used in British mines

• 1

INVENTIONS AND DISCOVERIES

• 18

• *c.* 1764 Hargreaves invents spinning jenny

• 1769 Arkwright patents spinning frame

• 1733 Kay invents flying shuttle   • 1779 Crompton patents mule

• *c.* 1784 Cort makes wrought iron using coal

• 1792 William Murdock lights his cottage with coal gas

• 1800 Screw-making machine invented

• 1815 Davy's safety lamp invent

IMPORTANT EVENTS

• 1771 Arkwright builds Cromford factory   • 18

1775–1783 Revolutionary War in America   • 18

1803–1815 Napoleonic Wars

• 1818 *Zollverein* formed in Ge

1845 The United States annexes Texas •

1854–1

1861–1865

BOOKS AND WRITERS

Charles Dickens (1812–1870)

Émile

Elizabeth Gaskell (1810–1865)

Edward Baines, *History of the Cotton Manufacture* (1835) •

ACROSS THE CENTURIES   EGYPT: THE OLD KINGDOM

4000 B.C.   3000   2000   10

Pharaoh Tutankh

Writing invented in Mesopotamia   Pharaoh Chephren   Abraham   Stonehenge built